# The Space Between
# Our Tears

*A Collection of Poems*

Marlet Cox Becnel

ISBN 978-0-692-10128-5

But these things I plan won't happen right away.
Slowly, steadily, surely,
the time approaches when the vision will be fulfilled.

If it seems slow, do not despair,
for these things will surely come to pass.
Just be patient!

They will not be overdue a single day!

*Habakkuk 2:3*

# DEDICATION

*To all who struggle to cope*
*with the difficulties and challenges of life*

There is always hope.

*For my nieces and nephews*
*Those here and yet to be*

You are our tomorrow
Your lives, our legacy

*For Terrence Michael*

In loving memory
You will forever own my heart.

# THE SPACE BETWEEN OUR TEARS

# INTRODUCTION

*The Space Between Our Tears* is the story of my heart's journey into the healing hands of God. I understand that all our journeys are different, but I believe we are all connected and that all paths lead to God. So as I open myself up to you, I pray you see yourself and realize that you too are on a journey of purpose, shaped by God. I pray that the truth and healing God has released in my life inspires you to discover your own—motivating you to keep pressing forward in hope and drawing nearer to God as He reveals himself to you and, therefore, you to yourself.

I pray that you begin to see and understand that the healing and peace you so desperately desire is within you and not outside of you. It does not exist in another person, place or thing. Though you may identify with my painful moments, by God's grace, I pray my healing will resonate more deeply—igniting or reigniting the flames of hope and extinguishing the agony of despair and hopelessness that haunts us all.

I pray these poems become tiny lanterns in your spirit, illuminating your path and leading you to the home of your hope and peace, which is always and only found in God. I lay my soul bare before you, so you will see my journey as evidence of the miracles God can perform regardless of the situations life throws our way.

With this confidence in God, I am daring you to trust Him in the dark and difficult places and to keep hoping or to hope again despite your current situation or the ghosts from your past. I promise that your morning is coming if you can endure, with hope, that the One who calls the stars by name has not forgotten yours.

So, take heart, dear one, God has not lost track of you. He is unfailing, unrivaled and infinite, and He loves you deeply, wholly and completely. He wants you to know that everything will be alright as you learn to trust and hope in

Him. Slowly, steadily, surely, you are discovering and becoming who you truly are, and the world will be all the better because of it.

With the greatest love, always,

~M.

# PART ONE: SLOWLY

When I look in the mirror,
Who is it I see?
So many times I wonder,
Do I know me?

## Circles

As I tumble into the deep
I reach out

But emptiness is everywhere

My thoughts are wide spiraling
With no answers only questions

I scramble to understand without comprehending
Forever seems never and tomorrows duplicate yesterdays

How much longer before dawn must I wait?
Longing to long no more

As I keep beginning without ending
    and continue moving on
To elsewhere somewhere nowhere
Circling myself in search of myself
I am an island of confusion

Frustration is the tide ebbing at my shore
As patience tries to navigate my stormy seas

## Trying to Forget

The words have stopped
Just short of my mouth
Stuck in my heart
Slowly falling apart

My feelings are tangled up inside
As though they are trying to hide
Staying clear of my conscious mind
Afraid of the answers they may find

Stopping
Praying
Mindful of breath

Hoping I'll remember
What I'm trying to forget

## Adrift

Weary in spirit
Wounded and frayed
Battered by grief
Bruised and dismayed

Soul tears so deep
Only God can perceive
Burdens so heavy
Only God can relieve

I pray that God's love
Overwhelms and restores
Giving beauty for ashes
Tranquil seas at my shore

May God's very breath
Become the wind in my sails
So my heart now adrift
Finds the peace that prevails

## The Breeze

The breeze is moody and complicated
Passes by when it feels like it
Never comes when I need it most

The breeze is like you
Cold razor sharp
Cuts through me so easily
Without sympathy or remorse

The breeze is like you
Warm comforting
No summer sweat
On my brow now

The breeze is like you
No breeze at all
To curse me or calm me
Don't know where it goes

The breeze is like you

## Puzzle

Unusual in all its ways
Life has a way about it

Unfamiliar at times
Still I try to figure it out

And then it gets tougher
And I never know where I'm going
Or where I'm going to be
Or where I'm going to end up

But I don't give up
That's not me

I just keep trying
Even when I really don't get it

Will this puzzle remain unsolved?
I guess that's the mystery

# Winter

I am so empty

I've never been here before
All doors closed

I cannot take much more

Soul ever-reaching
Piercing air with my pain

Clouds are in the sky
But they won't release the rain

Where is my joy?
My eyes cry tears of snow

It's winter in my soul

I don't know where to go

# Deep

I've gone so deep within my secrets
I've hidden me from myself

The real me
The divine me
The woman God calls me to be

She is lost
Somewhere
In me

## Hollow

I feel hollow
Empty
Drop some love in me
And it might echo forever

## Again

This isn't déjà vu
I'm trying to understand
Why this keeps happening

It's happening again

A never ending loop
Same beginning at the end

My plan isn't working
So I'll try it once again

## Soul Swing

My soul is swinging
Going way up high
Coming down real low
Back and forth I go

Soul swing
Soul swinging

Soul swing
Soul swinging

Higher, higher I
I could touch the sky
Close to the ground
I can see patterns in the dirt

I'm clean I'm dirty
Swinging back and forth

Soul swing
Soul swinging

# Regrets

The distant beats of yesterday
A muffled sound I hear
Tinged with failure and defeat
Boldly crowned by fear

They've come together
Remnants of my past
Imprisoning me in anguish
For the die has been cast

Drowning in antiquity
The future I cannot see
I'm dead to the moment now
The past is my home somehow

I know this doesn't make sense
Enclosing myself within this fence
Where lies the graves of my regrets

I'm just not ready no not yet
To stay in darkness is my choice
Even in the light I could not rejoice

I can't bear to come face to face
With how I ended up in this place

## Decay

The past is hidden somewhere in me

I pretend it's far away
Recoiling at its touch

My soul retreats to its safe place
Deep within the belly of denial

Uncomfortably comfortable
Safe and unsettled

The scent of regret and disappointment overwhelms

I can smell the stench of their decay

## Abyss

What do you want from me?
Eyes as deep as an abyss
Where truth floats aimlessly

Do you remember the moment?
You lost yourself slowly
In bits and pieces

Signs of complicity are all over you
Denying the truth too many times
Soul contorted in knots of denial
Looking away pretending blaming

It is costing you everything

## Until

I gave my peace away a long time ago
Scattered among the ruins of my life
Hidden in the push and pull of a man's love
Buried deep within my children's happiness
Anchored in bills I struggled to pay
Mistakes I couldn't undo
All the people that hurt me
Yeah they got a little bit of it too

And now there's none left for me

I told my heart to bury the rest of it
Until every wave within me lies still
Until all the pain goes away

# Walls

Heart soul mind
Peace has become lost among us

Unanchored

Longing to find our way home
Fearing the pain of truth

Walls rise between us
Soul's voice is gritty and raw
It knows what we must do

Heart weeps frozen by its haunting cries
While mind pretends to hear nothing at all

## Tomorrow

Today is overwhelming
Full of too many hard and painful things

My eyes cannot see all that must be seen
So I wait as God puts away the sun
Setting my mind on the next horizon

New grace waits on the other side
Safe from who I am today

I will do better

Tomorrow

# Tangled

What is it
Suffocating my hope?

Impossibly tangled
At the end of my rope

A sky without stars
A cloud without rain
A rainbow void of color
No end to the pain

Is my happiness in it?
Is my joy found in him?

Is my peace in my wallet?
Is my hope in that thing?

## Fruit

Housed in the deep
Alive within soul
There is a child
Desiring to be whole

Crying out in silence
Pain is how she speaks
Telling of great sorrow
Of struggles and defeat

The keeper of many secrets
She alone was there
When that seed was sown
Reaping fruit she could not bear

## Lonely

Pain
Healing
Two sides of the same coin

Broken things are supposed to find wholeness
One isn't meant to exist apart from the other
Sometimes traveling in different seasons
But the two should always meet

A wound left lonely will weep

And until they embrace
There'll be no peace.

## Whole Again

Tears dreaming of waterfalls
Praying to run free

I swallow them whole
So no one will see

I close my eyes
They tell my secrets too often

What can I use to disguise
These ghosts that haunt
Trapped inside
Beating on the windows of my soul

I look away until they stop
Drumming in my spirit
To let them go
Let them be
Outside of me

So someone else can see
What I need
So desperately
Is to be whole again

# Do You Hear Me?

Little by little
Bit by bit
You are slipping away from you
Pulling apart from yourself
Not knowing what to do

Who is this stranger
Staring back at me?
Is the mirror mistaken?
I don't recognize who I see

Somewhere deep inside
I know what I should do
But I persist in this madness
My soul is black and blue

How awful is my pride?
No one can ever know
So this hole grows deeper
And further down I go

Pretending that I'm happy
Trying to avoid
Trying to ignore
Trying to fill this void

God do you hear me?
Do you know where I am?

Please help me
I'm holding out my hand

## Ache

This ache

People
Money
Things

Nothing seems to ease it
Or quiet its cries
Its appetite is insatiable
It is never satisfied

A hollow, bottomless void
What does it want from me?
I've given it everything

Except for the truth

# Heartache

I see you over there
My eye fixed on your soul
Watching what you do
Or aren't doing

I'm wondering why
Why you keep hurting me

You are the bullseye
Center of my heartache

But here's the thing
I can hear God saying
To let you be

And I'll discover
The root
The birthplace of my pain
Isn't in you

It's in me

## It's Me?

I know you
I love you

But I'm still afraid

I want you to hold me
I fear I will fade

Into the darkness

I can't walk away
Feet firmly planted

Yet I know I can't stay

Here in this spot
It gets deeper still

Fighting resisting
A war of the wills

Save me
Please save me
I want to be free

Who's holding me captive?

I think that it's me

## Push

Whispers of truth

Healing cries out
Longing to be born within me

Opaque hands of denial
Cover my eyes
As I do everything to produce nothing

Not moving beyond where I am
All things are in reverse
Lies become truth
And truth becomes myth
Stories of what could never be
Because I am not ready to know

Staring at blank pages
Preparing to write new tales
Pain pushes against every part of me
Urging me to see
To awaken

# REFLECTIONS ON "SLOWLY"

The poems in my "Slowly" season reflect the turmoil I experienced as I constantly struggled with life, trying desperately not to drown in a sea of ever-changing emotions and feelings. These are the poems I initially didn't plan to include in the book because I thought they were too sad. However, these poems reflect how my feelings dominated my thoughts and became all that mattered in any given moment. I had more questions than confidence in God; unknowingly allowing problems and people to overshadow His presence in my life. I actually believed that if the problem went away, then, and only then, could I be okay.

In a poem I wrote as a young teen, "My Destiny," I questioned whether I would ever find peace. At that time, I believed that people and things were the pathway to peace. I didn't really understand that perfect, lasting peace only comes from God. It's a gift that only He can give. Without this understanding, I would call out to God in despair, desperation, frustration and fear. I looked to Him to just take the problems away. I was completely unaware that so many of my problems originated within me and not outside of me. I consistently searched outside of myself for peace because, somewhere deep inside, I believed that peace was something that happened to me rather than in me.

I believed that happiness was not possible unless virtually everything and everyone in my life was okay. I did not realize that even when I could (rarely) get everything to align, the peace I had was a false peace, easily shattered. I waited for peace to come before I could be happy. The perfect order I waited for never came, because we live in an imperfect world with imperfect people. I was rarely at ease and constantly frustrated because people didn't miraculously behave how I needed or wanted them to. And because my peace was tied to them, it was completely and utterly unstable. I would be up when they were up and down when they were down. It was like constantly riding the waves and crashing over and over again.

It was exhausting. I was so intensely focused on what was happening around and outside of me that I wasn't paying attention to the war raging within me. As a result, I couldn't see the true lesson that God desired me to learn. I circled the same mountains a million times because I either didn't want to deal with the pain and kept pushing it away, or I was completely overwhelmed by it. This sentiment is reflected in the first poem in the "Slowly" section entitled "Circles." I describe how I was going in endless circles searching for me. "Slowly" seasons are the seasons of circles, where we set out searching outside of us for the peace we desire, only to discover that it was within us all along.

# PART TWO: STEADILY

The fog hasn't lifted
The sky isn't blue
The rain is still pouring
You're at the end of you

## Twisted Vines

I don't know how I'll get past it
Or how I'll make it through
All I see is suffering
Sky that isn't blue

Wringing my hands together
Thumbs at the temples of my head
Pacing back and forth
Heart consumed with dread

I have to trust God with it
Trust Him with this pain

He caused storms to stand still
He can surely stop my rain

Does this rain have a purpose?

Coming to wash away
All that doesn't belong
All that cannot stay?

Is He allowing it for a reason?
Is there something He wants me to see?
Things hidden in the deep?

Twisted vines at the root of my tree?

## Psalm 23

Moments in life
No one can explain
Some wounds so great
Our souls can't contain

What am I to do Lord?
With all of this pain?

I can't see the sunshine
I only see the rain

Why did this happen?
How could this be?
I didn't deserve this
Why Lord why me?

Struggling to understand
What cannot be understood

My mind is tormented
I cannot see the good

In deafening silence
God speaks to me
A still small voice answers

Psalm 23

# Pride

There is a great wall within

Pride is the stones
I am the foundation
I build on my own

I carry the blueprint
Work around the clock

I have all the answers
I'm both the key and the lock

Impressed by my fortress
Loving what I see
I realize at that moment

The wall is trapping me

## Worry

Why does worry consume me?

Robbing me of joy
Struggling to believe
Feeling as helpless as a toy

Why won't I fall into His arms?
Stand steadfast in His love?

Why aren't my eyes turning upward?
For God is high above

He promises great comfort
He promises His peace

But first I must decide
To lay these worries at His feet

# Breath

Were we the truth?
Or what I wanted the truth to be?

Did I see you with closed eyes?
Your spirit withheld from me

Hiding in the shadows of what could have been
My tears fall in dry places
Turning dust into mud

I cannot bear to go that way again

Longing for the softness of grass underfoot
Warm sun kissing the nape of my neck
I exhale you

Inhaling me deeply
Until all of you is gone

All my breath restored

## The Sun

Grace walks with me
As my world falls apart

Lifting my head
Restoring my heart

I know it will get better
My tomorrow will come

Even in this darkness
I'll keep looking for the sun

## Once More

At times we struggle to believe
Whether God will come through

Persistent problems ever looming
What are we to do?

The sickness that won't quit
Bills we cannot pay
A marriage falling apart
Children who've lost their way
Loved ones gone too soon
Depression rotting within
Ghosts of past regrets
The secret weight of sin

Overwhelmed in mind
Pausing to take a breath
My heart quietly ponders

Has God failed me yet?

Remembering the seas He parted
The dead things He restored

All God has done
He will do once more

## Hope

Something just isn't right
Out of place in me
Desiring order but creating chaos

Knowing what I need to do
Yet unable to follow through

Deeper down I go
Failing to grab hold of knowing
Chance after chance emerges
Slipping like sand through my fingers

But at the very bottom of me
I can still see glimpses of light
Tiny slivers dance and dart across my hands

Hope is still alive within me

# Forgiveness

I remember how it hurt
When your pain tore into me

An undeniable TKO
Knocking me off my feet

And God was I angry
Wanting to give it in return
All the pain you gave me
When you left my soul to burn

But holding onto this offense
I withhold forgiveness from myself

To be forgiven I must forgive
The soul accepts nothing else

Forgiveness is a choice
One I tend to fret

You don't deserve it
Yet it's something I won't regret
Because at the other end
Of the thing I thought I couldn't do
Forgiveness is meant to heal me

It was never about you

## Faith

Problems problems everywhere
No matter where I turn
Over here over there
It's difficult to discern

Are You still with me?
Am I in this alone?
Is this fight even worth it?
Is this too far gone?

But rising from below
As worry gives way to toil
A mustard seed I planted
Is breaking through my soil

The soil of fear and disbelief
The soil of my pain

Somehow that seed took root

My sorrow was the rain

I marvel at its beauty
Tender leaves extend towards the sky

I had to first sow the seed
Now I know why

Faith is the courier
The messenger of belief
Working hand in hand
Joined as sorrow is to grief

Together they proclaim
Knowing not how or when
Against all odds God will deliver
This is not the end

So it matters not what I see
Matters not what I hear

Faith will slay the giant
It is the David to my fear

## Goodbye

I just needed some time to be sad
To think
About everything that had gone wrong

So we sat together for a little while
Regret and I

Allowing her pain to sink deep
Accepting it
Letting my heart break
As many times as it needed to

Over and over again
Until
I couldn't feel her weight on my chest anymore

I told her I didn't want to see her again
That I was moving on
And I had just come to say goodbye

# Pain

I stopped running away
And held you

Allowing every emotion
Every feeling

To live
To breathe
To expand

In my soul

## Heavy

Clothed in sadness
Threads of weariness and worry
Are woven throughout

Draped over my shoulders
Cascading like a waterfall
Pooling around my feet
Such a heavy garment

I cannot bear its weight
Because
It isn't mine

It belongs to my Father

## Ashore

Your waves are crashing over me
Overwhelmed, my soul cries out

Tasting only the saltiness of my tears
Falling asleep in surrender
I open my eyes

Standing
Watching
As you back away and disappear

Wet sand and broken seashells greet me
Tickling my feet
Causing me to remember joyful things

Awakened, I rejoice
I've washed ashore
No longer lost in your sea

I am home

## Tears

You're hurting
So you hurt me
But you can't dry my tears
Because you haven't cried your own

## My Story

I was not made in your image
Yet
You keep trying to change me
Mold me
Into who you want me to be

Slowly
Bit by bit
You are erasing my truth
Creating your fantasy

Sooner or later
I won't remember who I am
Lost in your story forever

I think it's time I write my own
Before I forget the words

## Shame

Shame looks at me with its deceitful eyes
Threatening to swallow me whole

Old secrets and lies are in its mouth

Its breath reeks of my past mistakes
Whispering of my unworthiness
Seducing me to bathe in the cold waters of regret

But I know who I am now

Hope is my compass

So I walk away
Further and further into my destiny
Where I no longer hear its voice

## Answers

Long forgotten memories
Secrets written in invisible ink
Inner chaos haunts silently

I don't know who I am
A terrible brilliant mess
Until parts of me collapse
Folding into myself

Fear burns in the fire of truth
Answers rise from its ashes

Sashaying circles of smoke
Disappearing once their dance is done

## Reborn

My love you are broken
So you break me

Strange sounds echo in deep valleys
As I shatter over and over again
Scattered by your pain
Pieces of me everywhere

White flags turn red
As promises with brief lives beg me to stay

But truth speaks loudest in the low places
She has come to take me to higher ground
Where broken things are planted and bear fruit

# Hidden

Emotions as boulders
Rolling tumbling about
Jagged edges pounding
Tender unknown parts

Old forgotten things
Called from the deep

Persistent pulling nagging

A loud quiet
Casting light in dark corners
Insisting I come to myself again
Remember who I am

God's glory
Hidden in me
Before I was born

## The Space Between My Tears

Oh the depth of sorrow
Painful echoes in my soul
Hiding from the light of hope

Threatening to take hold
Wandering in sadness

The emptiness of loss
Perpetual heartbreak

Thinking only of the cost

Through the veil of brokenness
God tells me He understands
The cause of my sorrow
The breadth of my pain

Holding me close
Sorrow looks from afar
As God counts every tear
And kisses every scar

The Lifter of my head
Slayer of my fears
Infinite and everywhere

Even the space between my tears

## Wake Up

I call out to myself
From within myself

Wake up

Move

You can't stay here
Lost in the illusion of temporal things
Singing their last songs at midnight

Bending truth like light
Creating many colors
Binding vines of despair

Where is my voice?

Crying out to my infinite self
It will lead me home
To freedom

## Judgment

It was just too hard
I couldn't carry it with me anymore
What you think of me
Your judgment
Those expectations

I had to let them go

Dry leaves
Devoid of color
Blown away by my truth

Now I can see my reflection in God's eyes
Who I really am
All that matters

# Love

To love you
Is to choose

Everyday

To see you as God sees you
Love you as God loves you

Whether it's easy
Or not so easy

Because if my feelings have their way

Some days
I would love you

A little
A lot
Or not at all

## Wisdom

There is a fork in the road

Choice mocks me in silence

Frozen with indecision
Watching as the seasons change
I surrender my will in springtime

The sun peeks through the clouds
Snow melts under my feet

Wisdom is leaping in my heart
God's word has arrived

Telling me the way I must go

## Palm Tree

Trouble is moving through the air
Bearing both pain and promise

The breath of storms
Ferocious and relentless
Charges at me

I am not prepared for this battle
But wisdom whispers
Embrace this temporary place
Even storms grow breathless

Surrendering to the rhythm of the wind
Moving as one
I dance to its music
It leads
Bending, not breaking me

Rooted in grace
I learn its secrets

Enduring
Until the music stops
And stillness returns
Blanketing the skies with blue and sunshine

Battered and bent over
I stand tall again
Stronger
Wiser
Triumphant

# REFLECTIONS ON "STEADILY"

Ultimately I moved into the "Steadily" season, which is where I grew weary of being sad and feeling lost so much of the time. This is the season where I finally decided to bear witness to my pain. I began to realize and accept that doing things my way was leading me nowhere, so I turned my focus inward and asked God to make me and my family whole. I had reached the very ends of myself, and this simple prayer started me on a path of painful but beautiful discovery.

God had begun the work of wholeness within me. I noticed that the more I tried to hang on to my husband or other people in my life, the more they seemed to push me away. I had not realized that these circumstances were pushing me towards God and towards my healing. The more I focused on God and what was going on inside of me, the more God exposed my brokenness.

With this recognition, I began to see a break in the clouds and glimpses of God's faithfulness. "Steadily" was the infancy stage of inner awareness where I was finally willing to face painful things and not run away from them or deny that they existed. I stopped blaming others for what I was going through, and I stopped waiting for something to happen outside of me to finally grab hold of the peace I so desperately desired.

Little by little, God revealed and peeled back those parts of me that were broken and did not serve His purpose for my life. I had issues with abandonment and codependency that I was completely unaware of, but once God helped me to identify those ghosts, my true healing began to manifest.

This stage of metamorphosis was difficult, but I knew, without a doubt, that facing all the things that hurt or scared me would lead me to my authentic self.

# PART THREE: SURELY

Bowing my head in surrender
To my God who lives within
He is the gateway
Peace is only found in Him

## Letting Go

No longer a need to understand
Or to be understood

I did all I knew
I gave all I could
Not giving up
Not giving in

I'm just opening my hands
Releasing what lies within

All the things I cannot control
The problems I can't fix
The fears that wake me at night
Loosened from my grip

I watch them floating up to Him
As I set them free

They belong somewhere else
They don't belong with me

At His feet my burdens lie
Pain and sorrow no longer in my hands
Renewed by His strength

I couldn't but now I can

## Scars

Vulnerability is
Where everyone can see
The real me

No mask
No pretense
Scars exposed
Every last one
Not just the ones I want you to see
Because then you wouldn't know the real me

Each one tells a story
Testifying from beginning to end
No pages torn out

They tell of the pain
Of how it began
And of the healing
So you know how it ends

# Grow

Hidden
Quiet
Guarded
Discreet

Insulated by the familiar
Comfortable
Secure

Then comes a whisper
God calling me out of warm and safe spaces
All so I could grow

## Reflection

There was a time I didn't know you
You had become a stranger to me

I didn't know how to love you
Not the way you needed to be loved

I saw everything I thought was wrong with you
No matter how hard you tried
I made you feel like you were never enough

And now look at you
Full of dreams and sunshine
Hope and gladness turning up the corners of your mouth
Peace, dancing around in your eyes

I think to myself
As I walk away from the mirror
I finally see who you are

## Crumble

I breathe in God's grace
Exhaling
   fear
     worry
       shame
          disappointment
Anxious thoughts
   crumble
As God's Word
Hidden in my heart
Rises up against them

## Beyond

A tiny seed
Buried deep in mystery
Watered by hope

Sprouting in good soil
Roots emerge
Born into midnight
Unable to see the light of the sun

Relentlessly growing
Persistently reaching up
Certain
There is something beautiful
Beyond the darkness

# Holy

There is lightness
Buoyancy
Effervescing in my soul

It's not happiness
Shifting like the wind
No, this
Is not born of temporal things

Anchored in eternity
Beyond flesh and bone

Immovable
Infinite
Holy

This is Joy

## Stillness

The rare absence of noise
Where curious thoughts fall silent
And breath flows with hypnotic rhythm

Serenity greets me
Tenderly
In this gentle quiet

The space between spaces
Where God tells me
Everything I need to know

# Blooming

I told God I was grateful
For everything

And then my eyes fell upon a perfect flower
Its petals stretched wide
As though it were blooming
Just for me

## Embrace

Truth has come for me
She is holding my lies in her hands

Tired of dancing with denial
Weary of hiding in the shadows
I fall into her embrace
Holding her close

We watch as stars light up the night sky
Dispelling the darkness

# Grace

Today stretches out before me
Pregnant with unknown things
Whose time has come to be born

I lock hands with grace
She sits with me in the dark places
Together we step over shattered things
Pressing through fear doubt worry

Escaping temptation insisting I abandon hope
Her wisdom causes me to endure

I sense the pain of scrapes and burns
Throbbing of my bruised heart
Casualties of the day's debris

Her strength shines through my weakness
Holding me together as today begins
        to sing its eternal goodbyes
Promising to be at my side in every tomorrow

## Home

My thoughts are passing by

Watching them as they go
Filling my head with truth and lies
I don't know what I know

Am I worthy?
Am I enough?
Am I a failure?

Should I give up?

Constantly searching for answers
Bouncing between two ends

Not bearing any fruit
Not sure I comprehend

Yet God gently assures me
That I'm worthy I do belong
There's nothing I have to earn
His love is my home

# Free

The voice of fear is loud
Telling giant lies
That I cannot do it
That I won't survive

The problem is too big
The sin is too great
There's nothing I can do
Give up because it's too late

The voice of God is bigger

His Word is clear
To us is given soundness of mind
And not the spirit of fear

Knowing in whom my hope abides
And that God hasn't lost track of me
I no longer run from fear

His love has set me free

## He Knows

God hasn't lost track of me
No matter the place I'm in
Be it basking in His glory
Or bathing in my sins

He knows all my secrets
He knows about the lies

He knows why I'm angry
He knows what makes me cry

He knows that I'm scared
He knows that I'm confused
He knows that I'm lonely

He walked to Calvary in my shoes

## Restored

Lord I need you

I long to be whole

Like the woman with the issue of blood
I believed you would restore

So much inner turmoil

You heard my soul's cry
My prayer touched your garment

I was healed as you passed by

## Trust

Fragile in faith
Melancholy in song

Yes I am weak
But Lord you are strong

Divine perfect power
Not born of men
The sweetest grace
Revealed in my sins

No burden to lift
Time to let go

Trust and be still

Know that I know
He who is
Who will always be

I am forgiven
Already set free

## My Friend

Not only to hope
But to deeply believe

Your grace is sufficient
It both calms and relieves

Disrupting sadness
Dispelling pride
Breaking yokes
Turning tides

Small steps forward
Through torrential rain

God is my friend
His grace holds my hand

## Truth

Truth is a beautiful certainty

Immortal at birth
It cannot be undone

Enduring and unchangeable
Never forgetting who it is

Unblemished by lies and shame
Head held high and steady

Bringing both joy and sorrow
No line to cross but its own

Bearing the weight of all things

Existing within the cascading silence of life

Denial falls quiet at the sound of its voice
Whispering what I've always known

# Victory

I can do this
I can make it through

I know I believe

I trust in you

Walking in your grace
Despite how I feel

Spirit always higher
I know you are real

So when storms threaten
I no longer run in fear
Charging boldly towards them
I am the lion not the deer

Confident because I know
I'm not in this alone

The battle was never mine

Victory is my home

## Horizon

Settled on eagles' wings
It's all below me now

Lifting ever higher

Trusting Him I vow
To push through the disappointment

To believe despite pain
To press forward in faith
To see sunshine beyond the rain

Soaring through the sky
I can finally see

Just over the horizon
Is who I'm going to be

## Flowers

Mountains rise high above the earth
Interrupting the reach of the sun

In their shadows pain masquerades as hollow
As though nothingness lies beyond its grave
Where hard things are buried deep

Yet these strange seeds bear fruit
Blossoming with the fullness of healing

Flowers growing about seas of rock and gravel

Persistent beauty
Unfolding ever reaching
Every petal praising God

Thankful for hard beginnings and beautiful endings
Their sweet fragrance lingers in the wind
Rising far above every mountain top
Whole and free

## Who I Once Was

Soul aches rooted in the deep
Thorny paths lead to wisdom
My feet are red with blood

Yet joy is everywhere within me

The mirror tells a new story
Reflecting the hidden things
Pain reveals me to myself
Her purpose dries my tears

Standing tall atop this knowing
Peace illuminates my night's sky

Winding roads hug the mountainsides
Where I was broken and reborn
Odd pieces fell away

And I am who I once was
Grateful to know her again

## Gratefulness

An ever-unfolding miracle
Profound peace has taken its rightful place
Contentment cascades as waterfalls
Free-falling into everything I will be

A river ripe with possibilities and promise

The world is old yet brand new
Gratefulness bursts forth from underground
Spiraling and rejoicing with new-found purpose

My soul rejoices in freedom
Soaring high above broken chains

## Peace

Joy bursts upwards into endless blue skies

Absolute gladness falls like confetti
Scattered everywhere within spirit

Thankful for the beauty and the ashes
Calloused hands greet in prayer
Grateful for the company of grace

Peace has found its home in my soul

# Rain

Opening my arms wide in surrender
I welcome the abundance of rain

Embracing all that I am
The divine sweetness of truth settles on my lips
As healing washes over me
And the past puddles under my feet

I search the heavens for rainbows

Clouds can't hide the sun forever
Its brilliant light will dance with the rain
Creating all the colors of hope
Stretching into infinity

## Finally

So this is the thing
Concerning that pain inside

It honestly felt awful
Yet I knew I could no longer hide

I wanted to run away
So much easier to deny
Pretend pretend pretend
It's how I'd get by

Running away in fear

God found me in the cave
Calling me to come out
It was time to be brave

Beyond the pain lies truth
It's the path we must take

It runs through the center
The middle of heartache

Finally one day

I stood eye to eye
Faced the unfaceable
Allowing pain to tell me why

Why I didn't feel worthy
Why I pushed others away
Why I was often sad
Why I wasn't okay

Pain revealed secrets
Things I tried to forget

Buried in denial

The fortress of my regrets

I listened closely
As hard as it may be
And pain told the story
Explaining me to me

Pain is the oyster
Truth is the pearl

Treasure we won't discover
Using the map of the world

Healing lies within
Buried deep but now I see
I was the answer

The big red X was me

## North Star

My soul lights up at the thought of You
Counting every hair on my head
My tears before they fall

I wrap myself in your spectacular love

You are my sun
My only North Star

Your sacrifice secures me
Your grace sustains me
Propels me
Into everything I will ever be

I love You

# Becoming

God I'm so grateful

I can't begin to express
My eternal gratitude
My heartfelt thankfulness

Your indescribable love so tenderly transformed
A wayward broken soul
A life lost in storms

Giving me hope
Placing angels at my side
Gently calling me out of caves
When all I wanted was to hide

Flooding dark places
With your eternal brilliant light
Assuring me through the pain
I would be alright

For as long as I can remember
Millions of times I prayed
Just to get a glimpse
Of what I see today

No longer held captive
By who I thought I should be
An ever-unfolding miracle
Becoming more of me

# REFLECTIONS ON "SURELY"

Oddly enough, my "Surely" season began at the gate of surrender. I surrendered my control, my will, and all my plans and expectations to God. I no longer tried to manipulate people or outcomes. I quit the juggling act and allowed all of the balls to fall. And when I did, my spirit, that part of us that is divine and who we were always meant to be, awakened.

"Surely" is my breaking out of the cocoon and becoming the butterfly. I soared with the absolute certainty that, come what may, I would always be okay, because God is ever-present and my suffering, although terribly uncomfortable at times, was not going to be wasted by God. This is when I became brave. As I surrendered and willingly faced and walked through my pain, I discovered peace waiting on the other side. To be clear, the problems didn't magically disappear—rather God's presence and predominance in my life grew so strong that I faced them head-on as never before.

"Surely" is where we accept and grow in God's gift of grace, understanding and believing that we are more than conquerors in Christ. We believe that if God is for us, no one can be against us. We believe that we are freed from our sins by the blood of Christ and that we need no longer carry the banners of shame, guilt and unworthiness. We know who we are because we know who He is. We no longer easily fall prey to the stories that our eyes and ears may tell us. Rather, we hold tight to God's promises and believe that no matter what, come what may, because God is with us, we will always, always prevail.

Today, I see God not only as my Savior, Helper, Protector, and Friend but also as a doting, loving Father. My time with God became less of me asking Him to help me out of this or to get through that and more of an expression of my love for Him and walking in radical belief of God's power and majesty. Our relationship is evolving to my loving Him because of who He is and what

He means to me rather than what He can do for me. It's falling in love but in a way that is beyond what I can express with words.

I know that in spite of my past, my failures and my mistakes, He loves me deeply. There is nothing for me to earn, He loves me just as I am. His love is not tied to how good I am or am not. It's a love like no other, and with this great love comes the certainty and comfort of knowing that nothing is impossible for God. Absolutely nothing!

# AFTERWORD

### My Destiny

As I sit alone
I think of days gone by
I wonder what my future holds
Where does my destiny lie?

I wonder how my life will be many years from now
Will I make my dreams come true?
I always wonder how

Will obstacles stand in my way?
Is the path clear to take?
Will I make it through each day?

These thoughts haunt my dreams
They linger within my mind

Will I have a happy life?
Is it peace that I will find?

I wrote that poem over twenty-five years ago, long
before I encountered the challenges and difficulties of
adult life. As a young teen, I was already questioning the
road ahead and pondering what life had in store for me.
Yet I could have never imagined the wild and winding
road I would travel in my search for peace.

Nevertheless, those dark, lonely, sometimes gut-
wrenching, and breathtakingly beautiful roads inspired
me to write this book and share my journey with you. I
always knew God captured every tear and that no part of
my pain would be wasted, that it was not meant to be kept
to myself, but that my story could possibly encourage
someone else. However, the manifestation of this dream is
so different from what I could have ever imagined.

I first imagined *The Space Between Our Tears* as a book

of hopeful poems that would uplift and inspire. Although the purpose remains the same, the final version you see before you is deeply, deeply more personal.

My entire manuscript changed when I read a number of other poems I also wrote over twenty years ago. I confess that many of them were very difficult to read. The poems revealed so much vulnerability that I could easily recall the depth of pain I was trying so desperately to relieve by transferring all those difficult feelings from my heart to the paper. Writing poetry gave voice to my sorrow in ways nothing else ever really could. I knew I should share them, but I struggled to figure out how these poems could possibly fit into a book intended to provide hope. They certainly weren't hopeful, rather, they gave voice to many moments of despair, doubt and utter confusion. I didn't understand how they could possibly inspire and uplift anyone.

And then God helped me to see that my pain was as important to my journey as was joy, hope and peace. I understood that God wanted you to see the promise, but it was equally important that you see the pain. You see, I know what it's like to have life take your breath away in the worst ways, to wake up and have no idea how you will make it through the day or to wonder when things will change for the better. My pillow is not a stranger to my tears, and my mind has been assaulted by doubt, worry and fear. There were times I closed my eyes, wanting to disappear because the pains of life were relentless and, at times, too hard to bear. Once I cried out to God that if my hope was a flame, then my flame was flickering and dangerously close to going out. I was losing hope that anything was ever going to change in my life. The pain seemed to go on and on without any foreseeable end in sight.

Yet, without fail, when I thought all was lost, God used something or someone to renew my hope. *The Space Between Our Tears* is my way of passing the gift of hope on to you as a beacon that will shine God's brilliant light, exposing the shadows of your past to His beautiful grace and dispelling any darkness you may be facing in your life right now. The poems chronicle God's faithfulness as the common thread weaving through my pain, stitching me, holding me together as I moved through stages of acknowledging God as the true seat of peace and hope in my life.

From a place of great pain, slowly, steadily, surely, I found my way home to God, his peace and, ultimately, to my true self. Although we walk along different paths, I believe that the journey of "Slowly, Steadily, Surely" is a divine, universal truth that connects us and runs through all our lives. Though the story changes from person to person, God never changes, so the truth He exposes in one life resonates with another because all truth originates from God.

May *The Space Between Our Tears* ignite your hope, encouraging you to surrender your pain to God, trusting Him as He slowly, steadily, surely guides you to yourself so that you too may know the exquisite beauty, joy, freedom and peace of wholeness that is only found in Him.

# ACKNOWLEDGEMENTS

To my husband, Pernell, I am so honored and grateful to continue this journey with you as we become all God has destined us to be. I will love you forever.

Compelling crazy complex
Passionate perfect perplexed
Our love has been so many things
Looking forward to what's next

My first my one my only
The waves in my sea
My joy my hope my sorrow
You mean everything to me

So worthy of it all
The breadth of my love I give
You will always be my treasure
For as long as I live

Beyond the dust of the earth
Beyond the barriers of time
My love for you is infinite

I will always call you mine

To my sons, Ryan and Devin, I am eternally honored and humbled that God chose me as your mother. You are incredibly bright, joyful and gifted young men. I look forward to walking beside you both as you journey into futures shaped by God. I love you both more than any written word can express. Like God, my love for you is eternal, beyond the stars.

Bouncing beams of light
Pieces of my soul
Energies of God
Joys to behold

The love in your eyes
More times than I can recall
Called me from the deep
To keep on hoping for us all

The sweetest little kisses
Bearers of big joy
Transforming overnight
No longer little boys

I pray you walk upright
Boldly onward into God's great plan
Always finding his light
Reaching for his hand

Two priceless treasures
Love that is and will always be
Forever in my spirit
Forever parts of me

∽⧢∾

To Daddy, Momma, Gail, Keith, Charles, Darlene, Bryant, Rodney, Mark, Tina, Kim and Denise, thank you for your love and for always believing in me. I love you all infinitely.

Eternally bound together
Different but not set apart
Established by destiny
A picture in God's heart

Daddy tender and strong
There's nothing you wouldn't do
You are God's beloved
Our souls are full of you

Momma our bedrock
God gave far more than we deserved
Choosing you as our mom
May our lives honor yours

Beloved brothers and sisters
Eleven we'll forever be
An odd bunch to some
Imperfectly perfect to me

God's heavenly masterpiece
Colorful threads woven tight
Housed in the halls of eternity
Beautiful in his sight

To Jeanette, Jean, Cynthia, Celeste, Kim —thank you all for loving me, listening and giving of yourselves over the years whenever I needed you. God used each one of you in ways, big and small, to mold me, guide me and teach me in so many ways through the different seasons of my life. I'm grateful for each one of you. I love you all, always.

Soldiers of God
Assigned to my life
Through difficult seasons
You helped me to rise

Pushing me forward
As I carried my cross
Being a light
When I thought all was lost

Offering kindness
And some tough love
Beautiful spirits
Gifts from above

Grateful to God I'll forever be
That our lives crossed paths
On my journey to me

∽∾∾

Becky, thank you for being so kind and generous to me at a time when you were experiencing a monumental loss. If you had not come to my door that day, I don't believe I would've been blessed to connect with Gayle. I pray that God blesses you greatly for your generosity and selflessness. You are a sweet, beautiful soul.

Gayle, you have been a godsend—literally. I am certain God placed you in my path, and I am so grateful that He did. Your tender and compassionate guidance made this a wonderful experience. I pray this book is the first of many that we complete together. Thank you.

Higher calls out to me
Setting out towards who I will be

Fear is my compass
Marching boldly towards its flames
Doubt fades away
Conviction is born in its fire

Broken and blessed
Healed and whole

Surrender illumines my pathway
Exceedingly abundantly awaits
As God's purpose for my life
Rises above the horizon

# ABOUT MARLET COX BECNEL

Marlet Cox Becnel was born and raised in Louisiana where she currently resides with her husband and their two sons. Marlet has composed poetry for over twenty years.

*The Space Between Our Tears* is Marlet's debut collection of published poems. In addition to her poetry, Marlet is also authoring a novel loosely based on her life.

Made in the USA
Middletown, DE
15 July 2018